Postcards

FROM A

Loving God

POEMS

HOPE ANDERSEN

ISBN: 978-1-954614-91-8

Andersen. Hope
Postcards from a Loving God.

Edited by: Hannah Cohen

PipeVine

P R E S S

Published by Warren Publishing / PipeVine Press
Charlotte, NC
www.warrenpublishing.net
Printed in the United States

For Haldis

Author's Note

"Ooh Ah Point" and "Piece by Piece" previously appeared in *Awakenings Review*.

"Mountain Laurel" previously appeared in *A Time for Singing*.

"Chalk Messages" previously appeared in *Indolent*.

"Miraculous" previously appeared in *How to Remodel a Life: A Guide to Living Well with Alcoholism and Bipolar Disorder*.

All poems reprinted with permission.

Table of Contents

Postcards

When I do not move,
they come to me
like birds to seed tossed
on the ground.
Words climb into my lap
like a bold child,
kissing my closed eyes.
Images rising from the misty lake,
a tangerine sunrise,
blue heron against a yellow sky.
In the snow, cherry blossoms shiver,
puckering at the tips of black branches.
My love is a man of muscles and desire,
wrapped in a red blanket
and gazing at the stars.
I read them,
the postcards.

Morning Musing

The answers come
from within my heart.
What are the questions
but tattered moths at the window
hungering for the flame?
Dangerous questions:
Do they approve?
Am I enough?
Do I belong?
Questions that suck me
into self,
drenched in the gasoline of doubt,
and ignited by fear.
I'd like to be a monarch
sipping nectar
from the yellow pearls
of a zinnia's crown.
Drinking what has been freely given
instead of flapping my ragged wings.

In Concert

A symphony of butterflies plays in my garden.

They rise and fall like musical notes,
resting on the heads
of still-bright zinnias
burying themselves
in mounds of wild white asters.

Tiny butterflies chase
one another, darting
from flower to flower
on imperceptible wings.

The air shimmers as they dance,
a multitude glistening
under the crystal chandelier.

Only the orange monarch,
    larger than the others,
fans the air gracefully,
rests on a dark baton,
then flies away.

Mountain Laurel

The belled skirts, pink and dotted,
are like fairytales in blossom,
its buds like puckered nibs of frosting.
As a child,
I plucked the delicate dew-filled blossoms
and sipped from them
with my pinky finger lifted,
among imaginary tea party friends.
I learned years later
that drinking mountain laurel can be fatal,
its juice a sweet venom.
Yet I still wish on dandelion fluff and shooting stars.

Chalk Messages, 2020

The children leave little eclectic messages of Hope
on sidewalks that spread out like a fork's prongs
in our neighborhood:
faith not fear
don't worry, be happy
we are all in this together
decorated with rainbows and big flowers,
birds, sunbeams, and smiles.
A child's way of dealing with COVID-19.
Children bounce on trampolines,
ride their bikes,
wear halter tops and shorts,
missing friends but not school.
The makings of a happy memory.
The year summer came in March
and let them laugh, play, gaze at stars.
Those independent days
of bottle rockets and sparklers,
bonfires long before the Fourth of July.
I'd like to be a part of their Bliss
but I am too close to sixty-five.
It isn't Wisdom that keeps me wary,
or knowing the Facts,
because no one really does,
but feeling the Wolf's hot breath on my neck,
my dead mother reaching out across my dreams.

Memorial Day

As a child, I threaded crepe paper
into the spokes of my Schwinn bicycle,
and combed the plastic streamers
on my handlebars.
The paper snapped like fireworks
as the wheels turned around and around.
I followed the mute-red fire truck,
its lights flashing
along the streets pulsing with flags,
babies high on their fathers' backs,
to the cemetery on the hill
where the fallen lay
silent, except for the trumpet's call piercing
deep into the mourning sun.
Did I even know why I was there?
I know now.

Summer Song

In the meadow, the milkweed thrives
catching butterflies
in its soft hammock of leaves.

Goldenrod arches
over the banks of the pond.
A fisherman casts his line.

The sumac's fat crimson rattles
sound the warning:
weather is soon to change.

This summer has been sweet
but so short.
Golden days descend behind the mountains.

Eighty Degrees

Wispy little clouds like a school of fish
      swim across the morning sky,
            tops of trees lit like coral,
the world an ocean.

I take my patterned swimsuit down
      from the clothesline,
my beach towel covered with watermelon slices,
    both cold from the night's low temperatures.

It's a wonderful world I live in
where I can swim in eighty-degree water
while outside, beyond
the big windows of the pool
    the wind shakes the last leaves
        from the trees
and snowflakes fall like musical notes,
each one a carol.

How confusing it is
    to be human,
        to be caught between seasons.

If I lived in New England,
where the world is etched in white,
I'd put my bathing suit away.
Instead, I'd wander through the frozen fields
    tasting the cold wind in my throat
        my eyes, tearing,

not because I am sad,
but because it's eighty degrees in my heart.

Priorities

I wish I could have stayed here longer,
watch bees dive into the scarlet bee balm,
hover over its soft lemon skin.
I wish I could have listened to the wind
whispering in the trees,
the *thud* of small apples falling,
or watched a struggling worm
escape from a bird's beak.
Frogs gulp in the pond,
the fish snap at bugs,
leaving rings on the water.
Trees reflected stand on their heads,
trunks rise from a splash of green,
patterns etched in bronze.
Life moves quiet as moss,
ferns swaying, and swallows skim the air.
Peace sweeps over me.
Come, Night, with your thousand fireflies
and galaxies of stars.
I will sit and listen
until I slip
into the Deep Sleep.
I dare not stay.

Mimic

A human fingerprint mimics the rings
on the cross section of a tree.
The mountains layered in red,
white, and brown
mimic the rainbow flat
against the canyon bottom.
In the distance, the mountain chain mimics
my life's peaks and valleys.
I hear drums,
supplications from a high cliff,
the plaintive crying of black birds
wheeling across the blue marble sky.
I hear my husband's rhythmic breathing as he
      sleeps,
and the wind mimicking the waves.
Maybe everything mimics something else.
My life mimics the dreams I make,
the dreams mimic the stratified canyon rocks,
decades divided by color,
by stone,
by the mindset I bring.
Everything will be erased soon enough.

Still Standing

Ancient trees broader than the span
of my husband's outstretched arms,
and taller than the top of the canopy
into which they disappear,
stand like sentinels in the forest.
I press my hand against their rough bark,
thick with grooves and pocks,
say a prayer.
I hear nothing back,
only the heavy message that they have been
in this forest a long, long time.
Long before I learned how to walk and wander,
they mastered the secret of standing still.
If they could walk away now,
lumbering, gigantic,
shaking the earth with every step,
would they?
The trees are content to be
nestled in this quiet corner of the world
among mountain streams, ferns,
the pale white rhododendron.
Why move
when where you are is perfect?

The Hanging Fern

I came out to water the hanging fern
I've been neglecting
on the front porch.

I stayed to watch morning break,
a velvet gray backdrop
behind black silhouettes of trees.

Down the street, a dog's coughing bark
resounds, while here beside me,
the crickets ring like golden bells.

All it takes is stopping and listening
to hear the first bird of the morning,
to feel the cool air rising up from the earth.

If all I am asked to do today
is sit in my white rocking chair
and watch my neighbor's lights illuminate

as we dip slowly into a new day,
I will be audience to bird songs,
to banners of light, brimming clouds,

but honestly, I feel myself distracted
already, pulled urgently to move on.
The hanging fern shakes its dry leaves, sighs.

Lifelines

It is amazing how permanent life can feel
when I am here, in the moment.
That illusion persists as I gaze upon
striated mountains stretched across the horizon,
the *blip*, *blip* of the higher peaks
making a heartbeat,
a lifeline going forever on.

Millions of years have changed these stones.
I just don't see it.
I see one moment in time
when beauty is indelible.
I seek to capture it.
Beauty moves through me,
through space and time,
always changing.
I am perpetually shedding my former self,
moving into my new incarnation.

I am not enamored with permanence anymore.
I am not interested in stopping time
or looking back.

This journey fascinates me.
Finding myself,
losing myself.
Someday,
like the giant saguaro,
I will simply be a skeleton in the desert.

Connect the Dots

I chase butterflies,
watch the tiny blossoms on the lime tree
grow, feel the wind blow.
Wrapped in a blanket of gray clouds.

Connect the dots in our sky.
   Aquarius holds hands with Virgo,
making love on the mossy forest floor.
All life connected.

We had a ship in a bottle once.
Clever as it was, but
going nowhere.
Life was an origami ship,
   multiple sails catching wind
   like gills sifting water,
sending me across the ocean.

Now my dreams swell,
some I never knew I desired.
This is what I am talking about:
Me, in front of a giant oak.
   A small book in my hands,

sharing secrets.

Safe and Warm

A field of white cows
lying down on the cold ground.
They look like cozy sofas
with soft curves.
I'd like to snuggle up with one,
lift my face to the winter sun,
feel its warmth and watch
the cows' steamy breathing,
smell their musky smell,
a smell I've loved since
I was a child and hid in the barn
one night, curled up with a calf
and her mother.
I don't know what I am trying to say
on this cold winter day,
except that I feel safe and warm
in a crescent of affection.

I Could Talk About Your Love Forever

how it envelops me
like soft snow falling
on cedar branches,
silent and slow,
changing everything.

Clematis buds wearing fuzzy coats
cling to their vines
and wait to emerge as splendid,
purple flowers.

Life is waiting
for me to stop and notice
nothing is the same.

The clouds have lifted.
The sun dapples the landscape.
Shadows sweep over the canyons,
white wings brushing magic clear.

Passengers

I have never been here before
in this station, waiting
without longing that the train will arrive,
without wondering if it will come at all.
I am just waiting,
watching passengers like me
lugging their baggage.
A lady in a green felt hat
needs help with her suitcase.
A young man, no older than my son,
stoops down and lifts it for her.
I am that old woman.

We are all travelers,
the saying goes,
waiting for the next great moment to occur,
for the train to pull into the station
with its plaintive horn, silver
sleek as a summer snake.
Women's heels tap-tap on the pavement,
the big clock bongs,
the stationmaster announces
arrivals and departures.

Blackberries

It is peaceful here, enough breeze
for comfort. The pool filter croons
over the turquoise water.
Leggy irises shake their floppy ears
as yellow buses, fat with children,
squeal by, racing toward summer.
The robins are back. They've built
a nest in my hanging fern, again.
I don't mind.
We are all up to something,
just being who we are,
doing what we do,
even God. Especially God,
who I thanked today
for the sweet blackberries.

The Moment

Rain pours down metal gutters,
tinny, rapid rain
like fingers quickly signing.
What does it say?

Could it be as simple as:
I am rain.
I get things wet.
Life is so easily complicated.
I turn the most mundane
into twisted puzzles difficult to solve.

Daffodils rise from the earth
to blossom as yellow bonnets.
They do not question the early spring.
Robins return before I expect them.
While I predict doom,
they pull fat worms from the wet soil.

Be in this moment,
really be in this moment,
as the rain quiets to a murmur,
as a car speeds by on the slick road.
My husband's spoon *clinks*
against his bowl as he eats his eggs.

If all I ever have is this moment,
the heater blowing air into my room,
the sparkling lights,
a warm cup of coffee,
tissues by my side,
it is enough.

All There Is

Is this all that there is?
you ask.
Some would say so.
Not me.
All this is so much.
There is no need for more.
I cannot speak for you.
For me, it is enough
to feel the seductive sun, warm
after bone-chilling cold,
teasing me to peel off
my winter layers,
and leave my bare flesh to feel
Spring's lips.
The whole world bursts
with living.
Tiny purple bubbles of phlox
erupt into flower.
Every tree wears a veil.
Green leaves slippery
as they electrify the landscape.
Resilient robins,
their plump chests puffed,
announce, in case you hadn't heard,
a new day is here.
Is this all that there is?
you ask.

If it is,
it stops here
with this carousel of color and song,
with the magician's trick
of night, stars, moon.
I will clap my hands together.

Notes to a Buddhist Monk

You say I should simply feel this,
not run away from the taste of a bleeding lip,
a hunger so deep I cinch inside.
This has no name,
this thing that unhinges me,
leaves me hanging like a broken door.
I try to put my finger on it.
You put your finger over my lips.
Embrace it.
This is part of who you are.
Running like the wind both forward
and backward at the same time.
Impatient to learn the outcome.
Frightened to get the news.
How many like me waver
between living and dying,
or hope and despair?
I would love to be pink Muhly grass
giddy under an autumn sun.

Patchwork Day

The crickets are snoozing outside,
their washboard snores.
Soon it will be morning.

The dove will light a candle in the dark.
Piece by piece,
the patchwork day takes shape.

If I were a pioneer woman,
I would be dressed already.
Sleeves rolled up to the elbows,
and pounding loaves of bread.

I'd swipe stray strands of hair
from my face, and breathe
a steady sigh, watching

the full moon dissolve into the horizon.

Next

I don't know what will come next—

not in the next minute,
not in the next day or hour.
I don't know what will come

when I cross the threshold
into my next life on this planet
or later in the next world,
if there even is a next world.

Something needs to matter.
All the heartbreak and joy
we have been through
needs to have been for something.

Immortality

Night falls, a gray blanket
covering a sleepy world.

While I sit on the chaise,
our little dog lies on my feet.

The insects sing their squeaky chorus.
This is what always is.

A sliver of moon lights
the dark woods, where the trees

are anonymous and everything is obscured.
Hard to remember the light

that promises to appear.
Patiently I count the stars

move slowly through these hours,
take small steps along the path.

A familiar breeze rustles the roses,
lifts their sweet scent into the air.

If I miss one minute,
I will miss it forever.

If I treasure each second,
I may never die.

Mourning Dove

Long and low whistles,
messages sent out
into the morning,
a practiced repetition at dawn,
hollow but persistent,
breathing a hole in the air
where the other birds
chirp, cheep, and chatter
a cluster of small sounds.
The mourning dove is relentless
in her cries,
as if she calls for a child who strayed
or a lover who left her,
never intending to return.
Or maybe she sings this way
just because she can.

Mother Wings

Under the winking eyes of many blinking stars,
I made a wish because they told me to.

I wished that I would attain great wealth.
Immediately, an owl called out in the night,

Who? Who who are you?
the voice of my mother cried out.

I knew it was her,
or the Universe she had become in death.

I went inside to write at the kitchen table.
She followed me, settling by the window,

asking relentlessly
as an engine turning over,

who? who? who? who?
who, who, who are you?

I saw my folly and took back the wish
asking, instead, to savor what I have

which is much,
including a dead mother who appears now
and then when I most need her,
reminds me not to take myself too seriously.

Desert Flowers

Walking up the dusty trail bordered in gold,
my heart works hard,
reminding me that I am human
                              in this vast panorama
of cacti, mountains, and wildflowers.
How easy to be lulled into a false sense
of eternity.

            Nothing lasts forever.
Only the memory of the wind grazing
my skin, the sun warm
on my face and neck,
            the golden poppies thick as rivers,

threading their way beside the trail.

Another Chance

The cows outside are so fuzzy
that they make me laugh,
lying in the mud like marshmallows
on hot chocolate.
The silver sky promises snow
and a long nap.

Later, I'll sit by the fire
and read my father's old sermon.
I don't agree with everything he said,
but I get this—

God has given me a second chance,
a new chance every day.
Impossibly wonderful this life of mine.

Woodstock, 1969

My parents rented a house on Cape Cod
for the month of August.
Mother loved the golden, slanting light.
Faulkner light, she called it.
I hated her for not letting me go—
she let my older sister go—
to Woodstock.
She sentenced me to afternoons on the beach,
rubbing greasy, orange *Bain de Soleil* on her back,
eating cranberry ice cream,
fishing for flounder with my father, and catching eel.
I lay in the cool sand with a blond boy
I barely knew, necking,
letting him fondle my breasts,
and smoking a little weed.
I could hear the bands playing in the distant waves.
Joni Mitchell's sweet voice whispering in my ear,
You are a child of God.

Anonymous

It is enough
to steer a little boat in a sea of big boats.
I feel the waves rolling
underneath me.
I gaze at the net of stars strewn
against the night sky.
I taste the salt on my lips
and hear the seagull's call.
I journey down the white moon path
and rock to sleep.
What do the big boats have
that I do not?
Heavier anchors to hold them.
More weight to pull,
louder horns.
I am content to be close to the water.
I dip my hand in,
laugh with my dolphin friends.
I am one whose name
you will never know.
My boat is called "Anonymous."

The Postcard

I found it in my drawer today,
a postcard from my father.
He wrote it years ago
on a trip to Spain.
He sent his love,
delighting in his journey,
made all alone since Mom was already gone.
He wrote in his long, precise hand
that life had served him.
He didn't say it served him well,
or long,
closed by offering a prayer
with promises to meet on his return.
We met once,
then wrapped him in as many coats as we could find,
though it was October and still warm,
drove to the airport on the hill,
and gazed out at Mount Anthony
in burnished gold.
All I have left of him,
aside from a few medals and some photographs,
is this yellowing postcard
sending his love.

There Are So Many Things That Could Happen

Right now. The mist that has wrapped itself
around the houses and trees,
like the silver scarf I just loaned a friend,
could vanish.

The sun, gone hunting elsewhere,
could suddenly break through—
a golden trumpet of light
in blue.

This foggy day
everything muffled. Lovely
wet, black trees arching like dancers.
The horizon a soft gray cat.

A very small part of me hopes
everything stays muted.
Am I truly ready
for change?

Forgiven

Bars of light rise up
from behind the dark eyebrows of clouds.
I feel my father's unforgiving glare
as though I had done something wrong,
which, of course, I had.
Hand in the cookie jar,
or stealing my sisters' things—
dolls, underwear, blouses, books.
I even took my grandmother's green felt hat.
Where did the impulse to steal come from?
To take what was not mine?
Prometheus, that clever trickster, stole fire
 from the gods.
Eve, the seductress, plucked the apple from the Tree.
Both caught, as I never was.
Desire smoldered in my heart,
where I had nothing and wanted everything
but didn't know the *How.*
Today I look at the sky
and see strings of light
from harp-shaped clouds.
I hear the stillness settle.
I taste the minty breeze and the ocean's salt-sweet mist.
I see fuzzy bees curled up in lime blossoms,
and the zinnias, once brilliant,
now brown and dying while asters bloom.
Everywhere I look is *Now,*
and I have been forgiven.

The Twelfth Step

At the zoo,
a herd of turtles
lumber up to me
where I stand,
capturing their deliberate parade on film.
The leader, ominous,
opens his marble eyes
and hisses.
His ragged jaws wide.
I recoil.

On a beach somewhere,
a sea turtle wrapped
in rope and plastic bags
accepts his fate,
until a loving soul with a sharp knife
frees him.
His feet slap the sand
as cold water tickles his toes.

He spreads his wings
and flies into the sea.

At the Feeder

The finches take turns
at the feeder outside my kitchen window,
yanking sunflower seeds
and shaking their heads
as if the seeds were too hot or cold.
The males have red breasts.
The females, gray.

I have had a headache since my ex-
husband telephoned me.
The birds extract the meat
from the seeds,
spit the shells onto the patio.

In the garden, daffodils outnumber tulips.
Forsythia glares.

At the feeder, chickadees descend,
fat as fists,
chasing the finches away.

I will have to ask him not to call,
though it isn't his voice
that hurts me.

Primary Purpose

While sitting in my comfortable chair,
the thought comes to me:
I will not be here forever.

Blood swells in my chest
and expands like a balloon
dangerously close to exploding.

This is no heart attack.
It is my Life urging me
not to be complacent.

The dreams I have
must not be delayed—
the trip to England,

the next book,
family dinners,
vacations at the beach.

Nothing is too big or too small.
Not hugs, not compassion,
not gratitude for all I have been given.

The clock could stop
on any minute.

So Close to Losing My Mind

Diving into opaque water expecting it to be clear.
Above me, the air is exquisitely blue,
the sun a Golden King.
I sleep through most of it,
my arms pricked with needles,
parboiling my brain,
hands shaking like a rescued dog.
My legs wobble.
My mind confused.
The doctors shake their uninspired heads,
unsure of what has taken over me.
If it is not COVID-19.
It must be COVID-19.
Only it is not.
My mind is gibberish.
What can I give you for a crystal word
floating out for miles over a crystal reef?

Heart Over Head

On the sidewalk, a newspaper declares
A Dream Come True!
This is a dreamy morning.
The air effervescent,
light sparkling on the trees.
So why am I anxious?

A tiny red ladybug creeps across
a crepe myrtle leaf.
She is so small.
Her journey is so long.
True for us all, I suppose,
as the Greater Light shines on whom it chooses.

I used to think that God was in all things.
White crepe myrtle blossoms,
Queen Anne's lace,
butterflies in the meadow, the breeze—
but that was five minutes ago.
Now I feel that God is in my heart,
helping me choose how I respond to the world.

As I walk along the path,
being in the moment,
my heart over my head,
I imagine Eve walking in Eden
before she doomed us all to over-thinking.

I want to live with a mind
blank as a piece of white paper,
only focused on wind that sounds like falling water,
and ribbons of light
circling the ivy-covered oak.

Doubt

Lonely winds moan through marsh grasses,
swaying in supplication.
She feels their loss,

standing at the edge of the water,
her toes buried in mud.
She has smeared herself in sorrow.

A heron contemplates the gun-gray sky.
The sun opaque and glossy,
staring back with one eye.

She feels as if she is dying.
The heron lifts its wings like bellows,
stirring the salty air.

She watches Icarus ascend
while oysters click their tongues.

World Made Possible

Spring is gradually shading in.
Like a child with a crayon,
              nature does not stay
between the lines.
         She colors the lawn blue and violet,
dresses the sky in a pink haze
     of blossoms and purple clouds.
I think I'll paint my room a misty lavender.

When this sunny day curls into night,
I will remember how it was
to live in a world made possible
by weeks of rain.

Ooh Ah Point

So many books just sit on shelves
collecting dust.
Life passed me by
as I watched television
or streamed shows on my phone.
I've been there,
down the Facebook rabbit hole,
losing hours of my life
reading status updates by people
I barely know.
When I go to Vermont this summer,
I want to skirt the tourist traps,
ignore the outlets and stores.
Instead I hope to hike the trail
at Merck Forest,
trudge up the mountain
through an ocean of ferns,
to the sweet spot where I can see
all the way to Massachusetts.
To take deep breaths
as I climb the rocky path
to Lye Brook Falls.
Nothing makes sense anymore
except the flora and fauna,
orange mushroom tops
on rotting logs,
the sea of golden poppies in the desert,

the brilliant, white-capped mountain
keeping watch over Flagstaff.
I don't have time to tune out.
Who knows how much time is left.
I choose to spend it
at Ooh Ah Point,
gazing up at the teal and rose rocks,
home to the spirit kings of the canyon.

A Second Home

My house is fine,
comfortable, and strong.
I love its old wood and older tiles,
the hearth, the baths aching
to be restored.

But what if I had a second home
in the mountains,
under a leafy parachute,
sunlight sliding through branches
with whispers of waterfalls?
The hills a rhythm of blue.

Or if I lived on the beach,
the waves' translucent coils
curling and crashing and infinite,
as five sand pipers on toothpick legs
flee frothy foam.

What if I lived on the Moon
under the cashmere throw of the Milky Way,
a neighbor to countless winking stars?
I would leave my life behind
and see with new eyes,
no longer needing to treasure

every little thing.
To look down on the inky swirl
of an *aurora borealis*,
gazing toward galaxies beyond.

Lunar Eclipse, January 21st

The black tree is a sponge
soaking up spilled stars
on Night's face.
The moon once white as milk,
now darkened by Earth's shadow.
We are traveling at sixty-seven thousand mph
yet everything is still.

During the last solar eclipse,
we drove four hours to be in its path.
We sat on my sister's dock
wearing our NASA-approved sunglasses,
disappointed by clouds,
but there was a profound moment
when the birds stopped flying,
and the air went still.
That memory chills me,
or was it the thirty-seven-degree weather
I left my warm bed for?

How easily awe adjusts.
The moon now a giant pearl,
luminous against the velvet sky.
I imagine our little planet
hurling itself along, reckless
and determined.
Casting shadows, changing lives.

The earlier wind has died,
and we rest
in sleeping bags at midnight
wearing our hats and gloves,
watching the impossibly slow
eclipse,
hoping for shooting stars.
My nose is so cold it may shatter.

Silver Pennies

Look at you, Moon,
so round and white
against the morning's blush.
I cut you from silver foil,
glue you next to gold and silver stars.
You must have a silver penny
to get into Fairyland.
My mother collected pieces
of my favorite poems
for me to illustrate.
I'm told I was a difficult child then,
artistic and demanding, even today.
I'm a lean dog, a keen dog, a wild dog and lone.
Red wax dripped from the black mongrel's mouth.
A felt bird singing by pink tissue blooms.
I meant to do my work today,
but the brown bird sang
in the apple tree.
I don't remember more,
except the moon,
the foil moon,
above the silver pennies.

Poem for My Father

I wonder what the weather is like
up there on the hill,
if it is raining, hailing,
or impossibly green?
Do you feel it, buried as you are,
deep in the earth?
It seems such a shame
we all must go.
You to cancer, which brought
increased humility, bowing down
before your humanness.
The catheter, the loss of hair,
the necessary dependence on others
for the smallest things.

You were a lion once, heading the pack,
leading the glorious way.
Like St. Augustine you sinned,
and though you never gave up booze,
you surrendered to compassion.
My children might say differently.
They found you to be gruff,
exacting, irritated by their antics and noise.
What did they know?
They were small and unruly,
used to the squishy affection I bestowed.

They didn't know how to act
around a proper Englishman.

I knew.
I knew my father's hands,
veins popping beneath translucent skin.
He held me as I stumbled through life,
searching for my place in this world.
My father was no saint.
His companions: pride, lust,
gluttony.
Avarice, doubt.
Is doubt a sin?

He never doubted the sunset
or my mother's love for him.
He believed in pied beauty,
the glorious spreading of the wings.

If he were here now,
I'd tell him how much he gave me,
letting me tag along on the shirt tails
of his love for God.
I'd tell him he saved my life
when I was drowning.
I'd tell him how his life gave mine purpose.
He would raise his hand and say, *Enough.*
We've covered that. We've covered everything.

The Conversation

If I came face to face with God,
sitting this very minute
at our old wooden table
scarred and burned by casseroles and knives,
I might be inclined to tell Him no
need to be gentle with me.
But underneath my worn silk blouse
my heart would pound,
and I would plead
be kind be kind.

I am not afraid of Death,
it's losing Life that scares me.

A black void of no feeling.
Unbeing.
Ceasing to exist.
Like the space in my mind
when I can't remember something.

I would miss blackberry cobbler
hot from the oven.
Hugs from my children.
Spring birds early in February
breaking winter's shell.
The purple violets embroidering
a tender green lawn.
This isn't over yet,
the conversation between us.

About the Author

Hope Andersen is a poet, novelist, and memoirist. Her poetry has appeared in *The Awakenings Review, Indolent, Ink&Nebula, The Pangolin Review,* and *The Literary Yard*, among others. She has published one chapbook, *Taking in Air* (Kelsay Books 2018). She lives in North Carolina.

www.ingramcontent.com/pod-product-compliance
Lightning Source LLC
Chambersburg PA
CBHW021940040426
42448CB00008B/1170